"I'm going to put on make-up like Mom,

and earrings and pretty dresses!"

Original Korean text by Haneul Ddang
Illustrations by Hye-won Yang
Korean edition © Aram Publishing

This English edition published by big & SMALL in 2016
by arrangement with Aram Publishing
English text edited by Scott Forbes
English edition © big & SMALL 2016

Distributed in the United States and Canada by
Lerner Publishing Group, Inc.
241 First Avenue North
Minneapolis, MN 55401 U.S.A.
www.lernerbooks.com

ISBN: 978-1-925249-13-2

Printed in Korea

When Mom's Away

THE ART OF RENOIR

Written by Haneul Ddang
Illustrated by Hye-won Yang
Edited by Scott Forbes

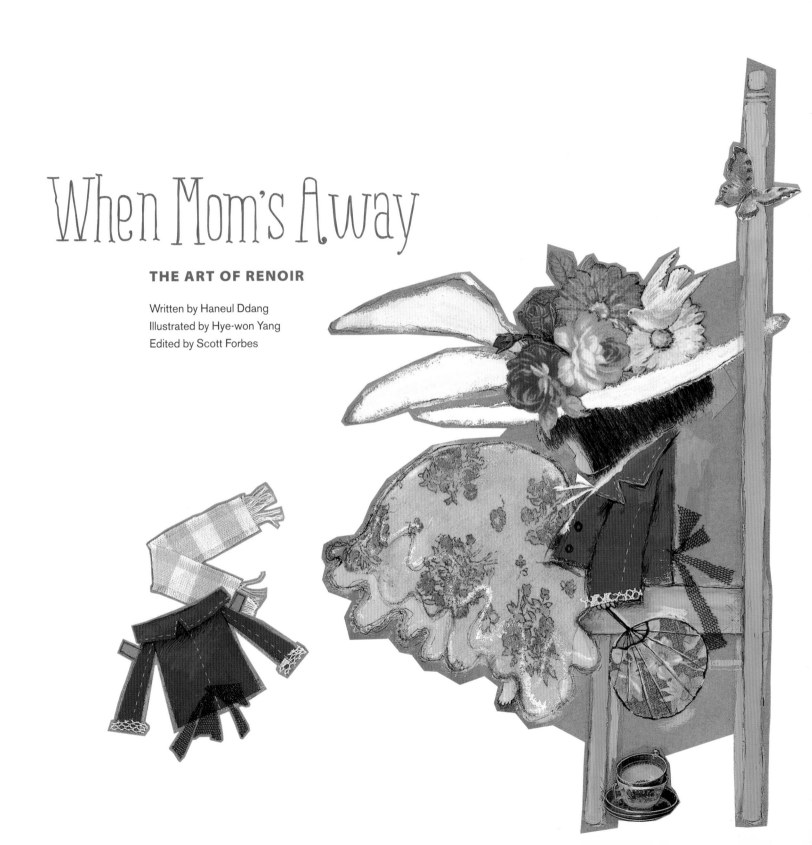

Mom is going out.

I'm reading a book.

I have to look busy so she'll be happy to leave me.

Has she gone out yet?

As soon as she closes the door, I can start.

So pretty, just like Mom

I put on make-up,
just like Mom — powder
and red lipstick.
I brush my hair back
and tie it in place
with a hairband.
How beautiful my hair is.
I put on dangly earrings.
I become pretty,
just like Mom.

Romaine Lacaux (1864), The Cleveland Museum of Art, Cleveland, USA

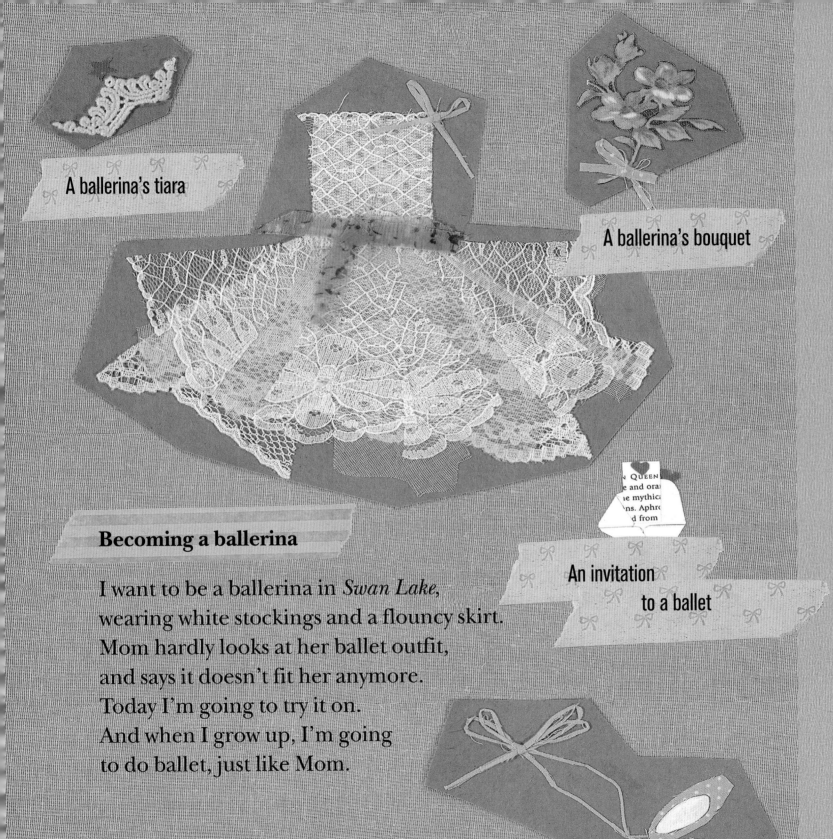

A ballerina's tiara

A ballerina's bouquet

Becoming a ballerina

I want to be a ballerina in *Swan Lake*,
wearing white stockings and a flouncy skirt.
Mom hardly looks at her ballet outfit,
and says it doesn't fit her anymore.
Today I'm going to try it on.
And when I grow up, I'm going
to do ballet, just like Mom.

An invitation
to a ballet

The Dancer (1874), National Gallery of Art, Washington, USA

❶ Mom's ballet outfit
I really like this skirt,
with its soft, lacy material.
I lift it up and it's as
light as the clouds!

❷ Belt
I used Mom's blue
summer scarf to
make a belt.
It will go really well
with my outfit.

❸ Bracelet
I've searched for all
sorts of bracelets,
but nothing looks
as good as my dog
Benji's collar!

❹ My sister's ballet shoes
My sister's ballet shoes
are a little big for me,
but I still like them.

❺ Necklace
Placed around my neck,
Mom's stretchy velvet
hairband looks like a
pretty necklace – even
if it is a bit too thick.

❼ Hairband
I roll up my lacy
handkerchief
and tie it around my hair.
It looks just right.

❻ Pantyhose
These are my favorite
white fishnet pantyhose.
This is the only part of my
outfit that belongs to me!

It's really pretty, but … I don't think I can go out like this!

13

I love to look beautiful

Next I'm going to dress like the child of
a rich, noble family — the daughter of
a prince, for instance, or a count.
I'll be like a girl in a fairy tale.
I'll wear a gorgeous dress
with beautiful lace trimmings.
Yes, that will suit me perfectly!

14

A Girl with a Watering Can (1876), National Gallery of Art, Washington, USA

❶ Elegant lace

I never realized how useful an old lace tablecloth could be! If I cut long strips from its edges, they make perfect trimmings for clothes. I'm sure Mom won't mind!

❸ Red handkerchief

This just looks like a piece of dress fabric. But if I roll it up and tie it around my hair it can be a beautiful ribbon.

❷ Polka-dot underskirt

This underskirt will be great for wearing underneath the black dress. It's my sister's, though, so it's a little big on me.

❹ Black dress

This dress was handed down to me by my sister. I never wore it because I don't like black. But I think I'll need it today.

❺ White ribbon
I found this white ribbon among Mom's clothes.
It's held on with a safety pin, so I have to be careful.

❼ Spray bottle
Now I need a watering can.
But we don't have any at home.
So this plastic spray bottle will have to do.

❻ Long boots
I don't have any long boots.
So I will have to borrow my sister's.

Actually, now I've got this outfit on, it feels a bit uncomfortable!

Now I'm a princess going on an adventure

I'm going on a journey with my falcon.
I'll wear a light, cool outfit, with loose
trousers and open sandals.
I'll use a yellow scarf to tie my hair back
and stop it flapping in the breeze.
I'll take some friends with me too.
Oh, I'm so excited about my adventure!

Girl with Falcon (1882), Clark Art Institute, Williamstown, Massachusetts, USA

❶ Flower
I needed a flower to
decorate my hair.
So I took a few from
the flower vase.

❸ Sleeveless blouse
This is Mom's summer blouse.
It doesn't matter that it's a little too big.
If I tie a belt around the waist,
It will look just like the one in the picture.

❷ Yellow scarf
This scarf is a little thick,
but if I tie it around my
head, it should look just
right.

❹ White towel
This is a little baby towel
that we don't use anymore.
If I roll it up tight, it makes
a great neckerchief.

20

❺ Dad's tie
This will be perfect for a belt. It's just the right length and color.

❼ Bracelets
I've borrowed some of my sister's bracelets. They are a bit too big, but they'll do.

❻ Flowery skirt
This is my sister's flowery skirt. The patterns on it are almost the same as the ones in the painting.

❽ Slippers
I couldn't find slippers like those in the painting. So I'll just have to wear my purple ones with the flowers on them.

My outfit looks good, but I'm almost tripping over the skirt!

21

Smarter than my sister

This time, I'm going to
look neat and elegant.
I'll wear a hat with
flowers on it and carry
a beautiful fan.
My sister always calls
me a kid, but in a few
years I'll be wearing
clothes like these too.
And then I'll look even
smarter than her!

Woman with a Fan (c. 1879), Clark Art Institute, Williamstown, Massachusetts, USA.

❶ Mom's hat
This is my favorite of Mom's hats.
I put a little flower on the brim,
and now it's perfect!

❹ Dark jacket
This is the darkest
of Mom's jackets.
It's similar to the
one in the painting.

❷ Flowery skirt
You can't see the woman's
skirt in the painting.
So I'll just wear my favorite
flowery skirt!

❸ Fan
This is a round paper fan that
my grandmother often used.
It's quite like the one in the
painting, isn't it?

❻ Brown shoes
I have shoes that are
the same color as
Mom's jacket.
So they'll be a good
match for my outfit.

❺ Blouse
This is one of my
aunt's old blouses.
The ribbons are a little
thin, but it will do.

24

I'm not sure I look as elegant

as the woman in the painting!

25

"Darling, what are you doing?"
I got such a fright when I
heard Mom's voice.
I turned around and there she was.

27

"Really, we should all dress like the women in these pictures, shouldn't we?" said Mom, smiling. Mom is so nice.

This dress looks like one from another painting.

All Mom's clothes are so pretty.

When I grow up, I want to wear shoes like these.

28

Two Sisters (On the Terrace) (1881), Art Institute of Chicago, USA

We dressed up together and went
out onto the terrace.
"We really do look like the women
in the painting," said Mom.
At that moment, Dad came home.
"Wow, you two look so pretty!" he said.
Mom smiled and then whispered to Dad,
"I don't think we can go out like this.
But perhaps you could make us
a special dinner?"

"It will be a dinner
fit for princesses,"
said Dad.

You see, I have an
awesome Dad too!

Celebrating moments of joy

Pierre-Auguste Renoir was born in 1841 in Limoges in central France, a place well known for its pottery. His parents were tailors and the family was not wealthy. Early on, Renoir showed talent in both art and music. Charles Gounod, a composer and organ player from the local church, advised Renoir to become a musician after hearing his singing voice. But Renoir preferred art to music, so his parents found him a place as an apprentice potter when he was 13 years old.

Valuable experience

Through his studies as a potter, Renoir gained valuable experience he wouldn't have had if he had only studied painting. In particular, drawing patterns on white ceramics taught him to create elegant, colorful shapes that he would later use in his paintings.

To develop his appreciation of art, Renoir visited major museums, such as the Louvre in Paris, where he studied the works of famous painters including François Boucher and Jean-Honoré Fragonard.

Girl with Falcon (1882), Clark Art Institute, Williamstown, Massachusetts, USA

Romaine Lacaux (1864), The Cleveland Museum of Art, Cleveland, USA
This doll-like girl is Romaine Lacaux. She was the daughter of the head of the pottery where Renoir worked. Renoir often painted pretty young girls.

Renoir's approach to painting

Renoir preferred to paint outdoors in bright sunlight because he liked to see people in natural surroundings. Renoir believed that paintings should always be beautiful and bring joy to people. So his works usually feature attractive people, especially women and children, in pretty settings such as gardens.

Working till the end

Renoir was a passionate artist who kept painting till the very end of his life. It's said that when his fingers could no longer hold a brush properly he had one tied to his hand so he could continue to paint. One reason why his work is so popular is that his passion for art is clearly expressed in his paintings.

A Girl with a Watering Can (1876), National Gallery of Art, Washington, USA

Two Sisters (On the Terrace) (1881), Art Institute of Chicago, USA
The women in this picture are not a mother and daughter as in our story, but two sisters. The painting was made at a restaurant called La Fournaise. The beautiful background in the painting later inspired many people to visit the restaurant.

1841
Renoir is born on February 25, in Limoges, France.

1845
Moves to Paris with his family

1854
Starts working as an apprentice potter

1862
Attends drawing and anatomy lectures at the National Art School in Paris

1874
Submits work to the first Impressionist exhibition

1881
Travels through Italy and develops his painting style further

1900
Receives France's most important governmental honor, the Legion d'Honneur

1919
Dies near Nice, in the south of France

"Oh dear, I've made the whole house messy!"